# Energy

## Use less – save more

## 100 ENERGY-SAVING
## TIPS FOR THE HOME

**JON CLIFT & AMANDA CUTHBERT**

Chelsea Green Publishing Company
White River Junction, Vermont

First published in 2006 by Green Books
Foxhole, Dartington
Totnes, Devon, TQ9 6EB, UK

First Chelsea Green printing July, 2007

Text design concept by Julie Martin, jmartin1@btinternet.com

Printed on 100-percent postconsumer-waste recycled paper

Printed in Canada

10 9 8 7 6 5 4 3 2 1   07 08 09 10

DISCLAIMER: The advice in this book is believed to be correct at the time of printing, but the authors and publishers accept no liability for actions inspired by this book.

**Library of Congress Cataloging-in-Publication Data**

Clift, Jon.
  Energy, use less—save more : 100 energy-saving tips for the home
/ Jon Clift & Amanda Cuthbert.
    p. cm.
  Includes bibliographical references.
  ISBN 978-1-933392-72-1
  1.  Dwellings—Energy conservation.  I. Cuthbert, Amanda. II. Title. III.
Title: 100 energy-saving tips for the home.

  TJ163.5.D86C58 2007
  644—dc22

                                      2007021274

Chelsea Green Publishing Company
P.O. Box 428
White River Junction, VT 05001
(802) 295-6300
www.chelseagreen.com

# Contents

# Introduction

> **Americans consume 26% of the world's energy.**

We are all using more and more energy: charging up our cell phones and laptops, keeping our rooms so hot that we walk around in short sleeves in the winter, or drying our clothes in the tumble dryer. But the consequences of using so much so freely is causing our climate to change and our energy bills to rise.

We're going to have to be more efficient in the way we use this energy. Most of the energy we use comes from fossil fuels, which when burned to produce the energy we all need releases vast quantities of $CO_2$ – the gas that's the main cause of climate change.

> **Our energy use is projected to increase 17% from 1995 - 2015.**

The energy we use in our homes comes from oil, gas, or electricity. We used to be self-sufficient in oil and gas, but now our reserves are drying up and we increasingly have to rely on foreign sources for our supplies: gas from Russia and elsewhere, and oil from often politically unstable countries.

The days of cheap energy are over – reducing our energy consumption is vital.

We can take control of this situation and reduce our energy consumption and our energy bills. We don't have to live shivering in an unheated room with no modern appliances; we're just talking about being more energy-efficient – reducing the need for so much power.

Little things that we can do every day can produce large results. If we all turned off our TVs and other gadgets that are kept on stand-by, for example, we could shut down a couple of power stations in the United States, with huge reductions in $CO_2$ emissions. Small actions, large results – it's really about being aware, knowing what we can do to have an immediate effect without compromising our quality of life.

> **18% of total emissions comes from operating our homes.**

Simple actions can considerably reduce our energy consumption and our energy bills and help reduce climate change: the less energy we use, the less $CO_2$ is released, which benefits us all. Once we are actually aware of what's happening, most of the things we need to do are just common sense.

# How much electricity do you use?

# How much electricity do you use?

The amount of electricity consumed varies hugely according to
which appliance and model you use. Check out the list below
to see which are the hungriest appliances. *All figures given
here are approximate – see your actual appliance for accurate
figures.*

| Appliance | Average watts used per hour | Appliance | Average watts used per hour |
|---|---|---|---|
| Low-energy light bulb | 11 | Iron | 1,000 |
| Extractor fan | 75 | Dishwasher | 1,000 |
| Laptop computer | 75 | Small portable heater | 1,000 |
| Conventional light bulb | 100 | Washing machine | 1,200 |
| Stereo | 100 | Stovetop (1 burner) | 1,300 |
| Television | 100 | Oil-filled heater | 2,000 |
| Video recorder | 110 | Fan heater | 2,000 |
| Refrigerator | 125 | Large portable heater | 2,000 |
| Desktop computer | 150 | Deep fryer | 2,000 |
| Freezer | 300 | Oven | 2,150 |
| Hair dryer | 750 | Electric kettle | 2,250 |
| Microwave | 750 | Demand water heater | 3,000 |
| Vacuum cleaner | 800 | Electric shower unit | 8,000 |
| Toaster | 1,000 | Stove (everything on) | 11,500 |

# Home heating

# Home heating

## Spend nothing – save money

**1.** Take control of your heating. Consider turning down the thermostat controlling the temperature of your room or house by 2°F. You will have either a single control at a central position, such as in the hall, or thermostats attached to the individual heaters or radiators.

**2.** Turn radiators off or down in rooms you use only occasionally.

> **WARNING – IF YOU ARE ELDERLY OR INFIRM, TRY TO KEEP YOUR ROOM TEMPERATURES NO LOWER THAN 65°F, AND YOUR LIVING ROOM AND BATHROOM AT ABOUT 70°F.**

**3.** You don't necessarily need to turn up the heating for babies: a room temperature of about 60°F–68°F is ideal.

**4.** Turn down the thermostat when you are going away on vacation: 41°F will prevent pipes from bursting in cold weather.

**5.** Set the timer for your heating system so that it comes on about 30 minutes before you get up and when you come home in the evening. Switch the heating off about ½ hour before you leave in the morning or go to bed.

**6.** If you use electric heaters, such as bar heaters, oil-filled radiators, or panel heaters, use them sparingly, as they are very expensive to run.

> **Heating and cooling account for about 56% of the energy use in a typical home.**

**7.** Move furniture away from any radiators or heaters to allow heat to get out into the room.

**8.** If you are too hot in your room, turn the heating down or off rather than opening a window.

**9.** Rather than turn up the heat, put on an extra layer of clothes.

**10.** Draw curtains over windows at night; they provide insulation and help to keep the heat in the room.

**11.** If your curtains are thin, line them with thicker fluffy materials, such as brushed cotton, to help keep the heat in.

**12.** Open the curtains during the day if the sun is shining on your windows, and let the sun heat your room.

> **Keeping our homes warm during the winter months accounts for about ⅔ of our household energy bills.**

**13.** Avoid covering radiators with curtains – they will funnel the heat out through the glass of the windows. Tuck them in behind, to enable the radiator heat to come into the room.

**14.** If you do not have double-glazing, you can reduce your heat loss by putting cling film over each window pane. It works very well, will reduce noise coming through the window, and should last the whole winter.

**15.** Keep external doors shut.

## Spend a little · save more

**WARNING – DON'T BLOCK UP AIR VENTS OR GRILLS IN WALLS IF YOU HAVE AN OPEN GAS FIRE, A BOILER WITH AN OPEN FLUE, OR A SOLID-FUEL FIRE OR HEATER. THESE NEED SUFFICIENT VENTILATION TO BURN PROPERLY – OTHERWISE HIGHLY POISONOUS CARBON MONOXIDE GAS IS RELEASED.**

**16.** Use weather stripping on your mail slot. It costs very little, but makes a big difference.

**17.** Fit weather stripping to external doors and windows. Foam strips are cheap, but if you can afford it, buy the longer-lasting rubber or plastic systems. You may not want to do this in your bathroom or kitchen if you have problems with condensation. *Make sure you still have sufficient ventilation – see above.*

About ¼ of all the energy we use to heat our homes escapes through single-glazed windows.

**18.** Stop drafts coming under baseboards or through floorboards by filling the gaps with strips of wood, cork, or the correct sealant. *Make sure you still have sufficient ventilation – see above.*

**19.** If your walls are not insulated, put some radiator foil between the radiators and the walls. It's cheap, very effective, and easy to install. Actual radiator foil is best; it has a layer of insulation behind the aluminum foil. Ordinary kitchen foil helps, but is less effective. Stick it to the wall with double-sided sticky pads, with the shiny side facing into the room.

**20.** Insulate your walls. If you have cavity walls, they are easy and quick to insulate, and in most cases it can be done in a day. Solid walls are insulated by placing cladding either inside or outside; it's more complex, but worthwhile, as solid walls lose more heat than cavity walls. *There might be a tax incentive to help you pay for this.*

**21.** Insulate your attic. This is probably one of the simplest and most effective methods of reducing your heat and energy loss. Attic insulation should be a minimum of 10 inches thick. You can do it yourself. There are some very user-friendly materials available, but whichever insulation type you choose, protect yourself with appropriate clothing and a face mask. *There might be a tax incentive to help you pay for the installation.*

**22.** Fitted carpets with underlay will give you much more insulation than hardwood floors and will stop drafts.

**23.** If you use gas or oil for heating, install a condensing boiler. They are more efficient than conventional boilers and will save you money and produce less $CO_2$. *There might be a tax incentive available to help you pay for this.*

**24.** Service your boiler regularly – it will be more efficient and use less energy.

**25.** Fit a thermostat to every radiator. This will enable you to vary the temperature in different rooms.

> **Almost 40% of all the heat used to warm rooms escapes through the walls and roof space if they're not insulated.**

**26.** Block up any unused fireplaces to stop heat going up the chimney. You can stuff scrunched-up newspaper into the hole where the fireplace enters the chimney, or buy special balloons to put there. Both these methods are good because they still allow a little air to circulate, which is necessary to prevent dampness.

# Water heating

# Water heating

## Spend nothing - save money

**27.** Turn down the temperature of your hot water at the central heating boiler, at the hot-water tank (if your water is heated separately), or on your instant water heater. Don't waste energy heating water only to have to add cold water so that it is not too hot to use! 140°F should do it.

> Adding insulation to a low R-value water heater (lower than R-24) can reduce standby heat losses by 25%–45%. This will save you around 4%–9% in water heating cost.

**28.** You can use less energy by taking a quick shower rather than a bath. If you use a power shower, remember that in five minutes it can use as much energy as a bath.

**29.** If you want a bath, then why not share it with a friend? It's much more environmentally friendly!

**30.** Don't leave hot-water taps running – use the plug.

**31.** If your hot-water tap is leaking, fix it quickly.

**32.** If your hot-water heater is not insulated, get an insulating jacket – if not, about three-quarters of the energy you are buying to heat your hot water is wasted. Insulating jackets are not expensive. Buy one that's at least 3 inches thick.

**33.** If you don't have a timer for your demand water heater, buy one. Set it so that the water is heated only when you need it.

It's a myth that you use less electricity by keeping your demand heater on all the time. It's much cheaper and consumes less energy if water is heated only when needed.

**34.** Insulate your hot-water pipes. Insulation is cheap and easy to fit: clip it around any uninsulated pipes.

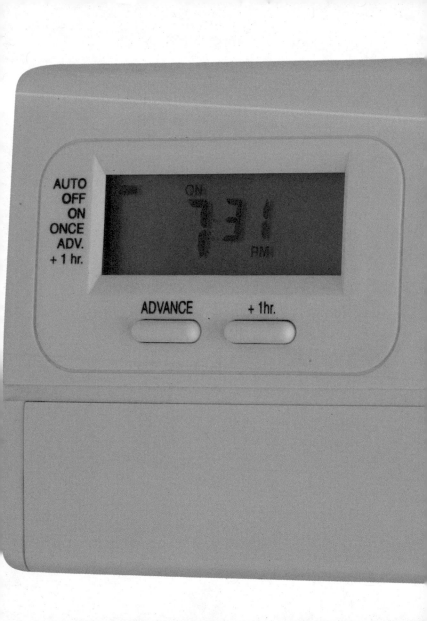

# Lighting

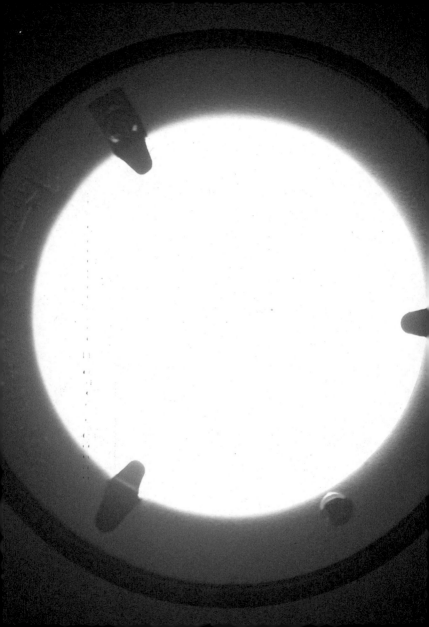

# Lighting

## Spend nothing – save money

**35.** If there's nobody in the room, or the room is bright enough without having lights on, switch the lights off. Get into the habit; it costs nothing and is really simple and effective.

**36.** Use natural light where possible.

**37.** Beware of torchieres (upright floor lamps): many consume a lot of electricity, using high-wattage bulbs of 300W or greater – that's the equivalent of over 30 low-energy light bulbs! Use energy-efficient spotlights instead.

**38.** Halogen bulbs consume less electricity than conventional light bulbs, but they generally need to be used in larger numbers because each bulb only lights up a small area, so you may end up using more electricity.

> **We spend 10% of our electricity bills on lighting.**

**39.** Have candlelit suppers.

*Keep fluorescent tubes on, or switch them off?*
Some people think that keeping fluorescent lights on is cheaper and consumes less electricity than switching them on and off, because to restart these lights uses considerable electricity. Restarting these requires some energy, *but only very little*. If you're going to be out of the room for more than a couple of minutes, switch them off.

## Spend a Little - Save More

**40.** Use energy-efficient light bulbs, as they last about 12 times longer than ordinary bulbs and consume about ⅕ of the energy. They come in all shapes and sizes, including spotlights.

> Energy-efficient light bulbs are cheap to run because they mainly make light rather than heat. 90% of the energy used by traditional bulbs is wasted in producing heat.

# Cooking

# Cooking

## Spend nothing – save money

**41.** Select the correct saucepan size for the heating element or gas flame.

**42.** Cut food into small pieces before cooking – it will cook more quickly.

**43.** Put a lid on top of the pan when you can; your meal will cook much more quickly, and you won't be wasting energy.

**44.** Use an electric kettle to boil water for cooking.

> Convection ovens warm up more quickly, distribute the heat more evenly, and use about 20% less electricity than a conventional oven.

**45.** Keep your kettle free of limescale – it will be more efficient. Fill it with a mixture of 2/3 water and 1/3 vinegar and leave overnight. Rinse it out well, fill it with water, boil the water, and throw it away.

**46.** If you are cooking with a saucepan, turn down the heat when it comes to a boil. You don't need as much heat to keep a pot boiling as you do to get it to a boil, and the contents will cook just as quickly.

**47.** Make toast in a toaster rather than under the broiler if possible.

**48.** If you're cooking vegetables in saucepans, only use sufficient water to cover them.

**49.** Consider using a pressure cooker for cooking some foods – it reduces cooking times dramatically.

> **Our demand for electricity grows by about 3% every year.**

**50.** 'Slow cookers' are a really cheap way of cooking. The cooker gently simmers away all day, using little more power than a conventional light bulb.

**51.** If you're cooking a meal in the oven, don't be tempted to keep on opening the oven door to see how it's all going, as you lose a lot of heat doing this.

**52.** Plan ahead: get ready-made meals out of the freezer early enough for them to defrost without using energy.

**53.** If you are in a hurry, heat or defrost ready-made meals in a microwave rather than a conventional oven.

**54.** Don't over-fill an electric kettle: just put in the amount of water you want, but make sure you cover the element. You'll use less energy, it will cost less, and will come to a boil more quickly.

**55.** When cooking rice, turn off the heat 5 minutes before the end of cooking time, keep the lid on and let it finish cooking in its own steam.

**56.** Use a steamer for vegetables – you can cook two or three vegetables on one element or gas ring.

**57.** Make one-pot meals that only need one element or gas ring.

**58.** Use your oven efficiently by filling up as much of the space as possible.

**59.** Cook two days' meals at once in the oven and utilize the space. Reheating will use less energy than starting from scratch on day two.

**60.** When using a conventional oven, food will cook more quickly on the top rack – it is much hotter than the bottom.

**61.** Where appropriate use the grill rather than the oven.

## Spend a little - save more

**62.** Electric kettles vary in the amount of electricity they consume. When you need to replace yours, choose one with the minimum energy consumption.

> Electric kettles consume surprisingly large amounts of energy because they are used frequently, generally heat more water than is needed, and have to bring the water up to boiling point – an extremely energy-hungry process.

**63.** Check out microwave ovens. They consume about 80% less electricity than a conventional oven.

**64.** If you are replacing your electric oven, consider a convection model as they are cheaper to run.

# Keeping things cool

# Keeping things cool

## Spend nothing – save money

**65.** Wait until hot food has cooled down before putting it into the refrigerator.

**66.** Don't keep the fridge door open any longer than necessary.

**67.** Keep fridges and freezers well away from heat sources such as ovens, dishwashers, and washing machines.

**68.** If possible, site fridges and freezers out of direct sunlight, as your appliance will use more energy trying to keep cool in the sun.

**69.** Try to keep your fridge and freezer full; they will use less electricity.

Refrigerators and freezers are never turned off – although they may not appear to use much energy, in an average home they are responsible for about 1/3 of the total electricity bill.

**70.** If your freezer isn't full, fill empty spaces with scrunched-up paper or bubble wrap to stop warm air circulating when it is opened.

**71.** Defrost food by putting it in the fridge the night before you want to use it. This will cool the fridge down and reduce its power consumption.

**72.** Keep the metal grids (condenser coils) at the back of fridges and freezers clean and dust-free and not jammed up against the wall; this allows the air to circulate more easily around them and makes them more efficient.

> A chest freezer uses less electricity than a front-opening model because the cold air doesn't fall out every time the freezer is opened.

**73.** If you have a custom kitchen with a built-in fridge or freezer, make sure there is ample ventilation to allow for air circulation around the condenser coils.

**74.** Defrost the fridge and freezer regularly. If the ice inside is thicker than 1/4 inch, the appliances become inefficient.

## Spend a little – save more

**75.** Consider buying an energy-efficient freezer to replace older appliances. You should recover the cost remarkably quickly.

**76.** Check the door seals on your fridge and freezer: shut the door on a dollar bill. If you can pull it out easily, or if your seals are damaged, they need replacing.

> **A new Energy Star®–labeled refrigerator consumes about ⅓ of the electricity of some of the older models.**

Energy Star® is a joint program of the U.S. Environmental Protection Agency and the U.S. Department of Energy helping us all save money and protect the environment through energy-efficient products and practices.

# Washing and drying clothes

# Washing and drying clothes

## Spend nothing – save money

**77.** When washing clothes by hand, there is no need to have the water hot. Most non-greasy dirt will wash out easily with cold water and detergent. Cold water is fine for rinsing your clothes afterwards.

**78.** Wait until you've got a full load before using your washing machine – using the 'half load' program does not save you half the energy, water, or detergent.

**79.** Use a lower-temperature wash for clothes that aren't very dirty: for most washes, 104°F is just as good as 140°F.

> **Washing clothes at 140°F uses almost twice as much energy as a 104°F wash.**

**80.** Use the economy program where possible.

**81.** If your machine has a cold-wash option, try using it for lightly soiled clothing. Most detergents work extremely well at low temperatures.

**82.** If possible, connect both your hot and cold washing machine hoses to your hot and cold water pipes. This will enable the machine to use readily available hot water rather than having to heat cold water from scratch.

**83.** If you live in a hard-water area, limescale on your washing machine element will reduce its efficiency. Every couple of months get rid of it by running the machine empty on a wash cycle using 6-7 fluid ounces of white vinegar in the detergent tray. There are also de-scaling tablets available.

> Energy-efficient washing machines use about ⅓ less electricity than older machines. The savings will more than cover the price of a new machine.

**84.** Air-dry your clothes on clothes racks or lines if possible – tumble dryers are very energy-hungry appliances.

**85.** If you have to use a tumble dryer, spin dry or wring the clothes before putting them in it. Clean out the lint filter every time you use the dryer: this improves the efficiency and your clothes will dry more quickly.

**86.** Switch the tumble dryer off when it has finished. It consumes almost 40% of the power while on stand-by.

# Washing dishes

# Washing dishes

## Spend nothing – save money

**87.** When washing dishes by hand, fill a bowl with warm water and a little detergent, washing the 'cleaner' items first. Use cold water for rinsing.

**88.** If you use a dishwasher, wait until it is full before using it. Don't be tempted by the 'half-load' facility, as it is nowhere near as energy-efficient.

**89.** Use the 'economy' or 'eco' program if your dishwasher has one. It will use less electricity and take less time.

**90.** Switch your dishwasher off completely when it has finished; it is still consuming electricity on stand-by.

**91.** If you switch off the machine and open the door when the dishwasher enters its 'drying phase', the dishes will dry naturally, saving a considerable amount of energy.

When you buy a new appliance, get an Energy Star®–labeled model; they cost less to run, save you money, and contribute less to climate change.

# Electrical appliances and gadgets

# Electrical appliances and gadgets

Our appetite for electrical appliances continues to grow, as does, of course, our need for even greater quantities of electricity to power them. Refrigerators and TVs have become bigger as mobile phones, computers, iPods, and the like have gotten smaller. We now have electrical appliances in nearly every room of the house.

## Spend nothing – save money

**92.** Turn off the chargers for your mobile phone and laptop when not in use.

**93.** Turn off TVs, radios, stereos, and computers when not in use.

**94.** Turn your iron off just before you finish ironing, and use the residual heat for the last few clothes.

At any one time in most households an average of 8 appliances are left on stand-by. In the average household the TV is left on stand-by for more than 17 hours a day.

**95.** Use the Alliance to Save Energy's interactive Home Energy Checkup that provides instant feedback; the Environmental Protection Agency (EPA) and the U.S. Department of Energy (DOE) also offer interactive Web tools.

**96.** Use your electricity meter to see for yourself which appliances use the most electricity: have a look at your meter while somebody is switching on gadgets, toasters, tumble dryers, radios, televisions, etc.

> Smart Meters, which give 'live information' about the cost of electricity, gas, and water and also store details about your previous usage, are being installed in California by PG&E.

## Spend a little - save more

**97.** Think about buying a small portable monitor that shows you how much electricity you are using, how much it is costing, and the $CO_2$ you are adding to the atmosphere.

**98.** Buy a steam iron: although they use slightly more electricity than dry irons, they are more efficient and take less time.

> Most video recorders and cable boxes are never turned off. Even in stand-by mode they consume about 85% of the power that they use when working. Some appliances use even more than that.

**99.** If you are replacing your computer, consider a laptop – they are more energy-efficient.

**100. Spread the word!**

If you do nothing else . . .

Switch off the lights!

# Renewable energy and your home

Renewable energy is energy produced by a source that continually renews itself. Well-known sources are the sun, moving water, wind, and plant materials. This energy can be used for space heating and hot-water heating, and to produce electricity for your home.

By using renewable energy instead of conventional energy sources, you can reduce the amount of carbon dioxide your household produces. This will reduce your contribution to climate change and save you a considerable amount of money once installed, as most of these energy sources will provide endless free energy and reduce the impact of gas and electricity price increases.

Provided you have already taken some basic steps to reduce your energy consumption, there will probably be tax rebates or incentives available to help you pay for the purchase and installation of a renewable-energy system. These can be quite substantial

When considering the purchase and installation of a renewable-energy system, you need to consider:

**The suitability of your home**, such as: Do you have a south-facing roof or wall? Is your house exposed to the wind?
**Payback** (the amount of time it takes for the renewable energy system to pay for itself). This varies considerably according to which system you install.
**Initial cost** Some systems are dramatically cheaper than others to buy and install.

The following is a brief outline of renewable energy systems.

## Solar power

Energy from the sun can be used both to provide domestic hot water and to produce electricity for your home. Different technologies are used for each.

### To produce domestic hot water

Solar heating panels use the sun's energy to heat domestic hot water. This energy typically reduces your water heating bill by 65%–75%.

Solar heating systems work in conjunction with your conventional domestic hot-water system.

Most south-facing roofs, walls, or gardens are suitable for the installation of solar heating panels.

## *To produce electricity*

Photovoltaic (PV) cells convert sunlight to electricity. This electricity is fed into the main electrical grid, thereby reducing your electricity bill. The PV cells can be put on a south-facing roof or wall, provided that they are strong enough to support the additional weight and are not shaded by trees or other buildings.

## Small-scale wind turbines

### *To produce electricity*

Wind turbines convert moving wind into electricity. For many houses, a new breed of micro-turbine that attaches to your chimney or roof is the most convenient and practical.

The electricity produced by micro wind turbines is fed back into the main electrical grid, thereby reducing your electricity bill. Your house needs to be exposed to the wind to make this system suitable for you.

## Biomass (biofuels)

### *To heat your house and hot water*

Biomass or biofuels are materials such as wood or straw that grow quickly and can be burned to release heat for space heating and domestic hot water. Biomass is different from all the other renewable energy sources because the fuel generally has to be purchased.

Biomass is a renewable energy source because:
- The materials are quick to grow, absorbing $CO_2$ in the process.
- The $CO_2$ released when it is burned balances that which was absorbed during the growth of the material, effectively making the process carbon-neutral.

Wood (in the form of logs or pellets) is the most commonly used biofuel. It should be burned in an efficient, controllable manner, either in stand-alone stoves or in boilers.

## Ground source heat pumps

*To heat your house and hot water*

Heat pumps take heat from under the ground (which remains at about 54°F all year round) and use it to heat your house – just like a refrigerator in reverse. They can also be used to warm water before it enters your domestic hot-water heater, thereby saving on energy used. If you want to install a heat pump, you will need sufficient space outside to dig either a trench or a borehole.

Although heat pumps are run by electricity, they are very efficient: for every unit of electricity used to run the heat pump, about four units of heat energy are created.

## Small-scale hydropower

*To produce electricity*

If you are fortunate enough to have a fast-moving stream or river running near your house, it might be possible to generate electricity from the moving water. Though not the simplest of renewable energy systems to install, hydroelectric systems have the capacity to generate substantial amounts of electricity, which can then be sold back to your power company.

The potential source of power will need to be assessed initially before any other steps are taken. Costs of hydroelectric power systems vary hugely according to the size of the project, but hydro systems can sometimes offer high returns.

If you think your local river has the potential to generate electricity, consider forming a community hydro project. There are people operating successful systems who are willing to provide advice.

# Advice and incentives

There are many incentives, rebates, and tax breaks to help you save money. Information and advice are available to help you:

* Insulate your home
* Generate your own electricity and heating from renewable sources
* Improve your heating
* Purchase energy-saving appliances
* Generate electricity and heat for your community from renewable sources

Rebates and incentives are available from your energy supplier as well as state and federal tax incentives – and can be quite substantial, especially if you are considering installing a system to generate electricity or heat from a renewable source.

For advice and offers available in your region see the American Council for an Energy-Efficient Economy Website for a state-by-state summary of tax-incentive programs, and The Tax Incentives Assistance Project for information of federal incentives.  (See Resources.)

# Resources

## The Alliance to Save Energy

The Alliance to Save Energy promotes energy efficiency worldwide to achieve a healthier economy, a cleaner environment, and greater energy security.

Website: **www.ase.org**

## American Council for an Energy-Efficient Economy

The ACEEE is dedicated to advancing energy efficiency as a means of promoting both economic and environmental prosperity.

Website: **www.aceee.org**

## American Council On Renewable Energy

The ACORE works to bring all forms of renewable energy into the mainstream of America's economy and lifestyle.

Website: **www.acore.org**

## Appliance Standards Awareness Project

The ASAP is led by a steering committee that includes representatives from the environmental community, consumer groups, utilities, and state government. ASAP provides advice and technical support to parties interested in advancing state standards.

Website: **www.standardsasap.org**

## Consortium for Energy Efficiency

The CEE is a non-profit, public-benefit corporation that uses the power of mass markets to advance super energy-efficient technologies that benefit consumers and the environment.

Website: **www.cee1.org**

## Department of Energy: Energy Star and Energy Guide

ENERGY STAR® is a government-backed program that helps businesses and individuals protect the environment through superior energy efficiency; the Website offers comprehensive information about energy-efficient appliances.

Websites: **www.energystar.gov**
**www1.eere.energy.gov/consumer/tips/ energyguide.html**

## The Energy Foundation

The Energy Foundation is a partnership of major donors interested in solving the world's energy problems by advancing energy efficiency and renewable energy.

Website: **www.ef.org**

## Natural Resources Defense Council

The NRDC is one of the nation's most effective environmental-action organizations, which uses law, science, and the support of 1.2 million members and online activists to protect the planet's wildlife and wild places.

Website: **www.nrdc.org**

## The Tax Incentives Assistance Project

The TIAP is sponsored by a coalition of public-interest nonprofit groups, government agencies, and other organizations in the energy-efficiency field and is designed to give consumers and businesses information they need to make use of the federal income tax incentives for energy-efficient products and technologies passed by Congress as part of the Energy Policy Act of 2005.

Website: **www.energytaxincentives.org**

# THE CHELSEA GREEN GUIDES

CHELSEA GREEN'S NEW *GREEN GUIDES* are perfect tutors for consumers or businesses looking to green up their knowledge. Each compact, value-priced guide is packed with triple-bottom-line tips that will improve the environment and your finances. Slim enough to fit in a kitchen or desk drawer, you'll return to *The Chelsea Green Guides* frequently for concise, sage advice.